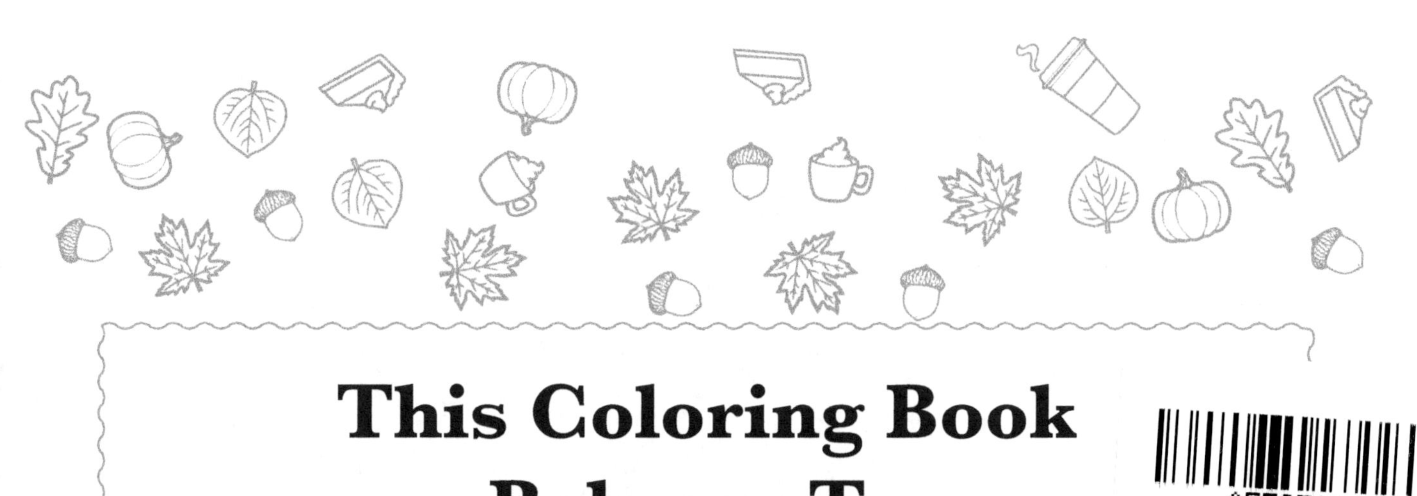

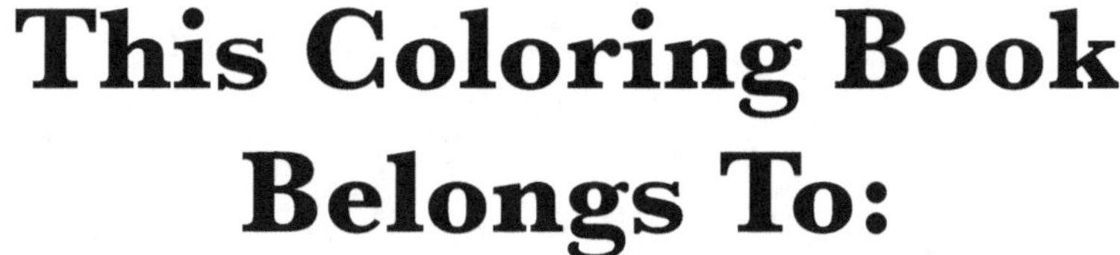

This Coloring Book Belongs To:

____

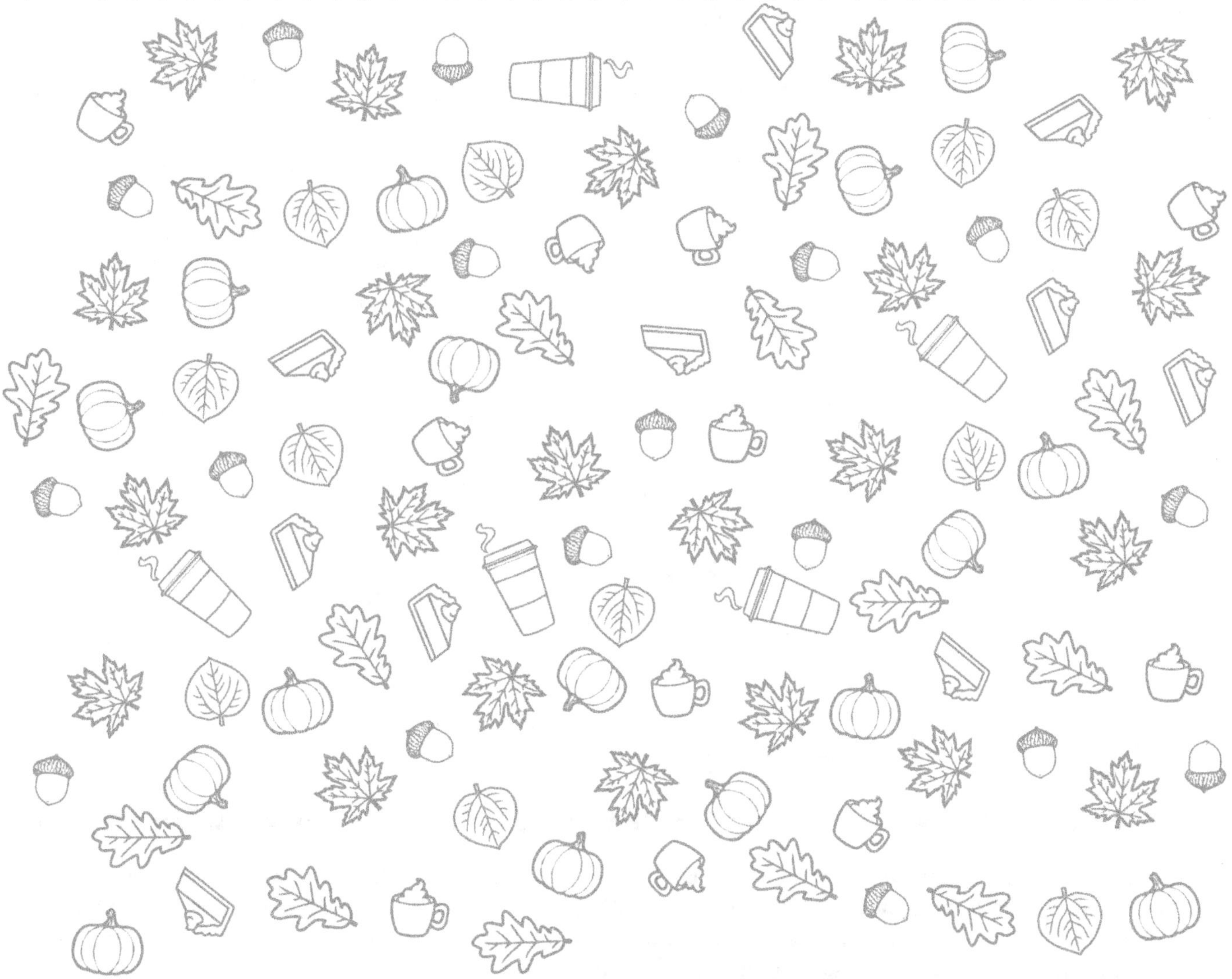

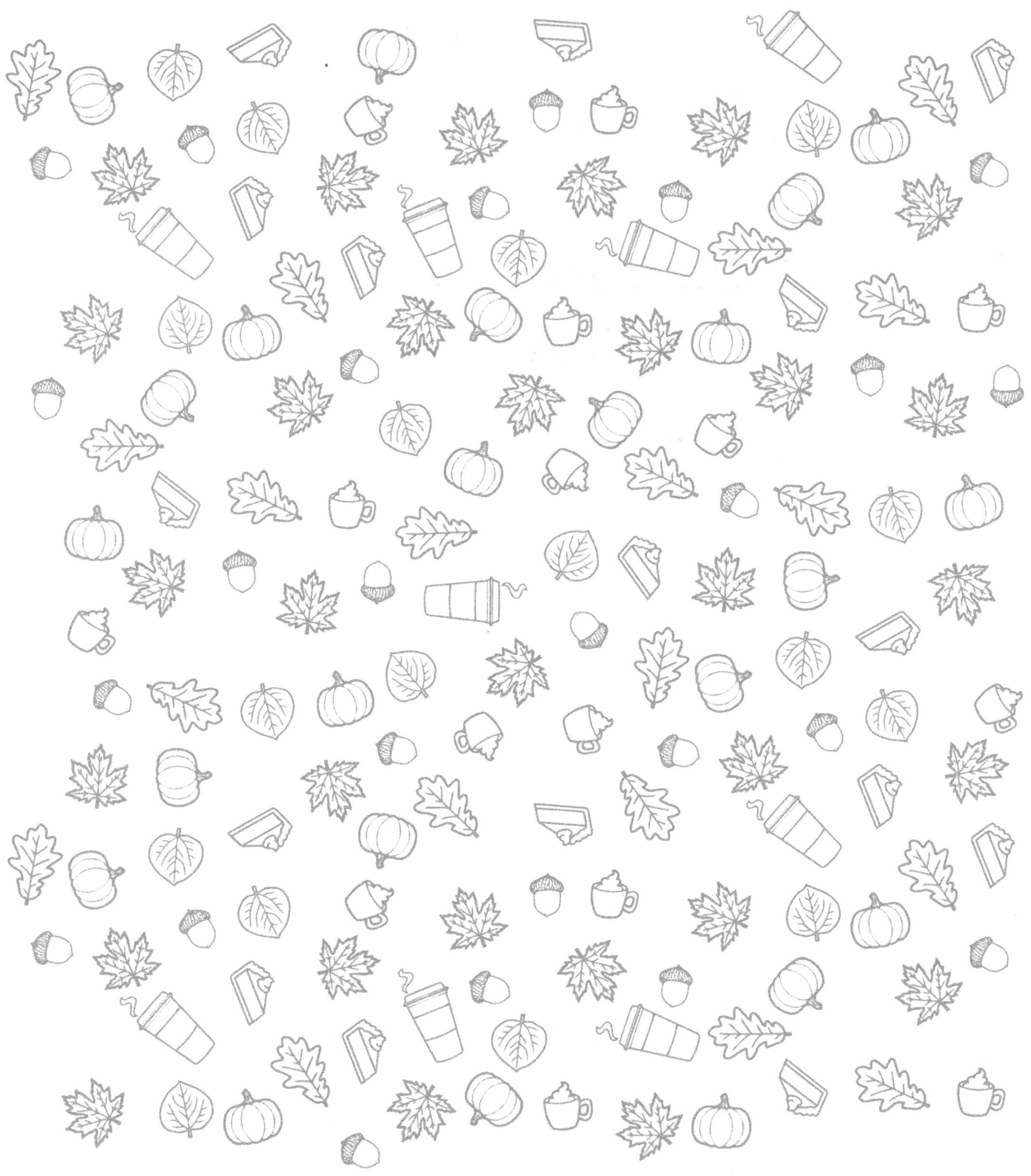

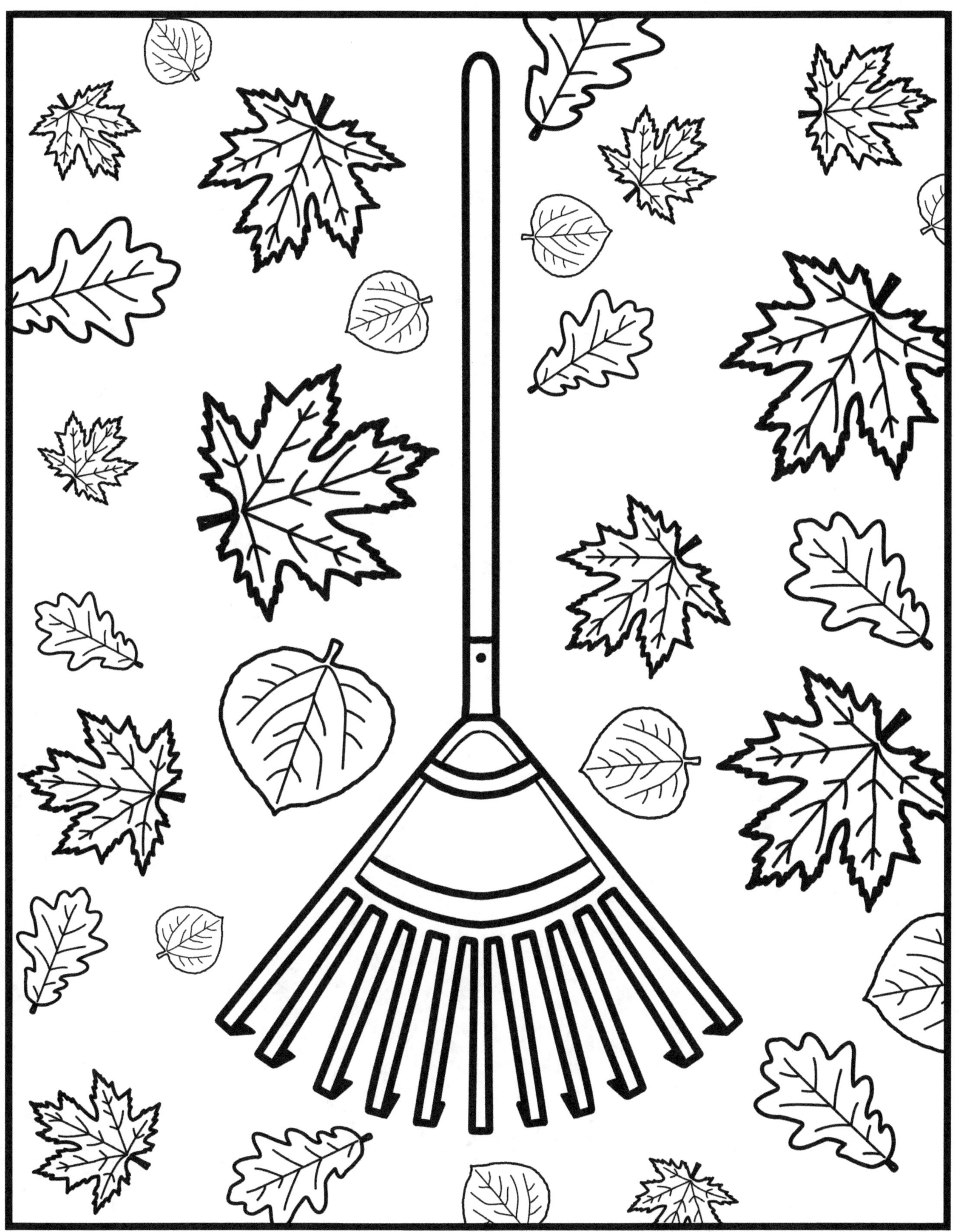

Rake It Up!

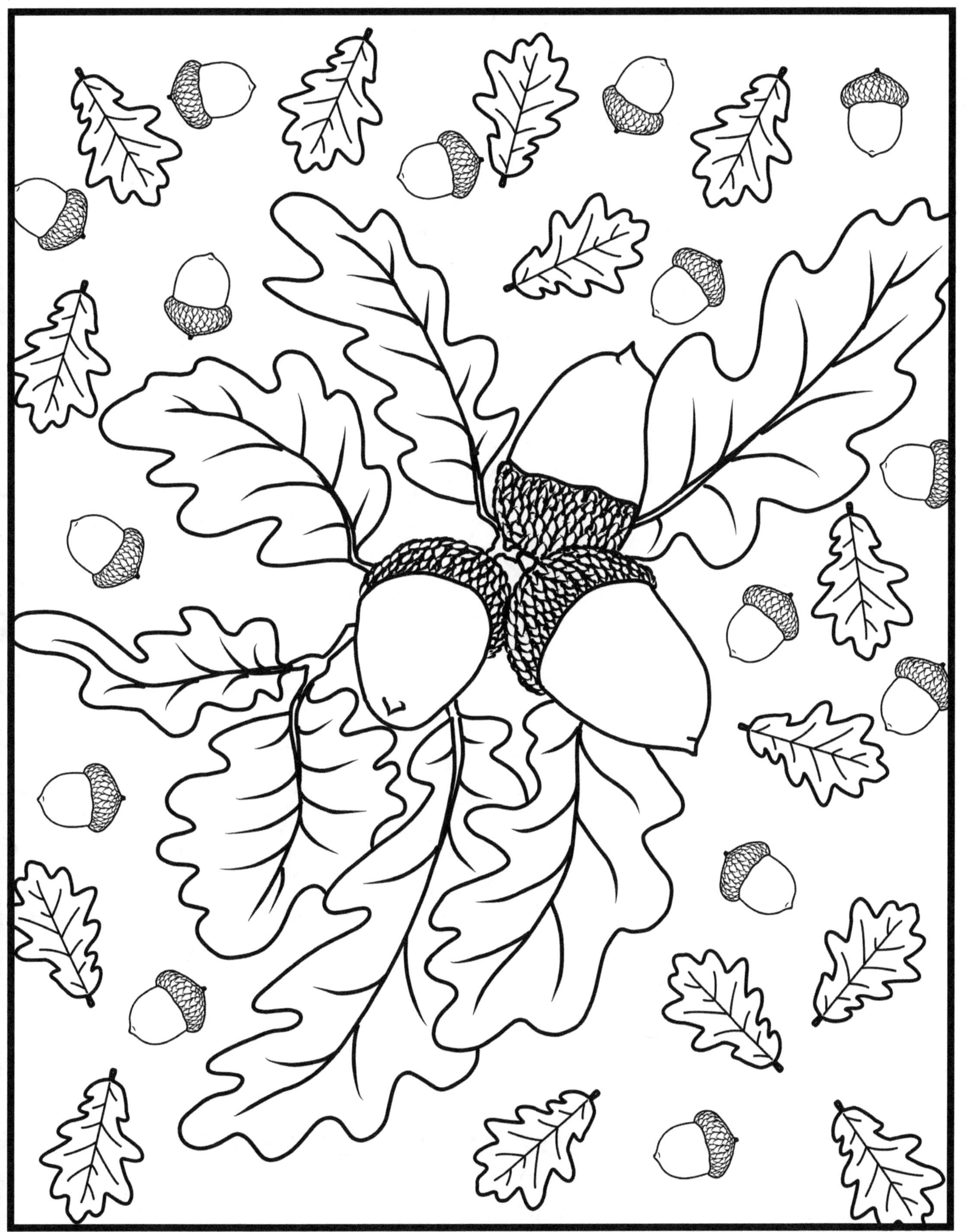

Oak Acorns & Leaves

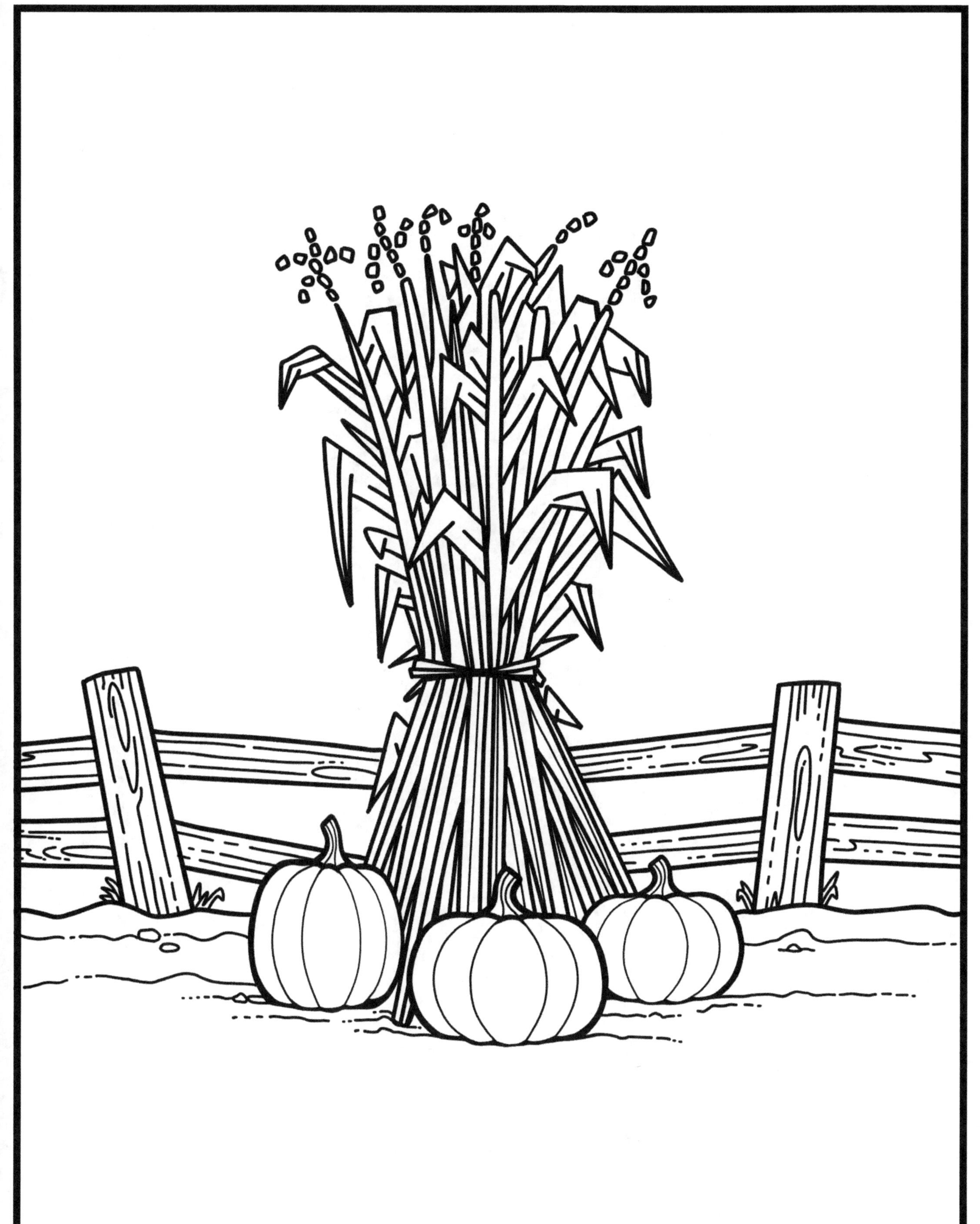

Corn Stalks

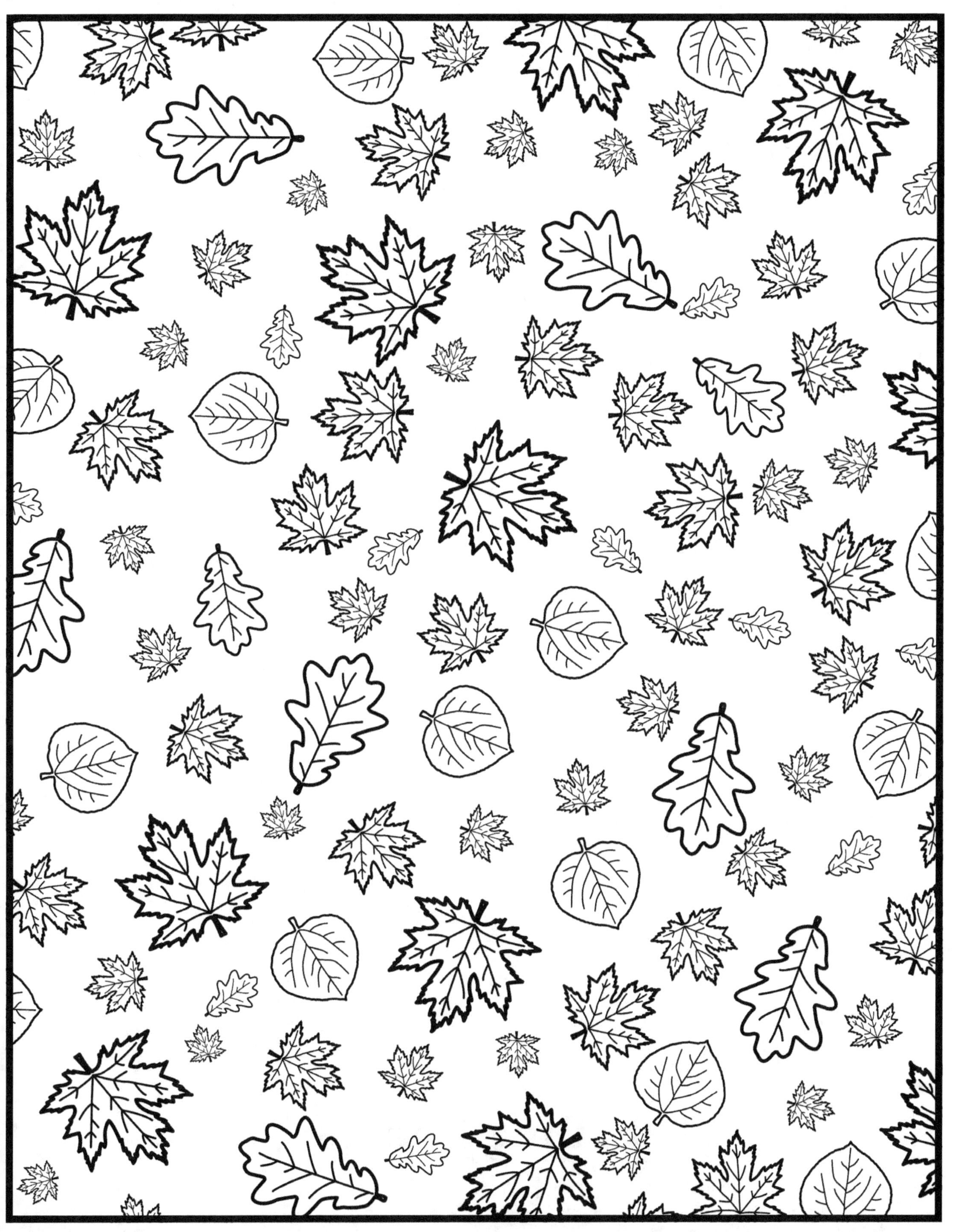

Falling Leaves

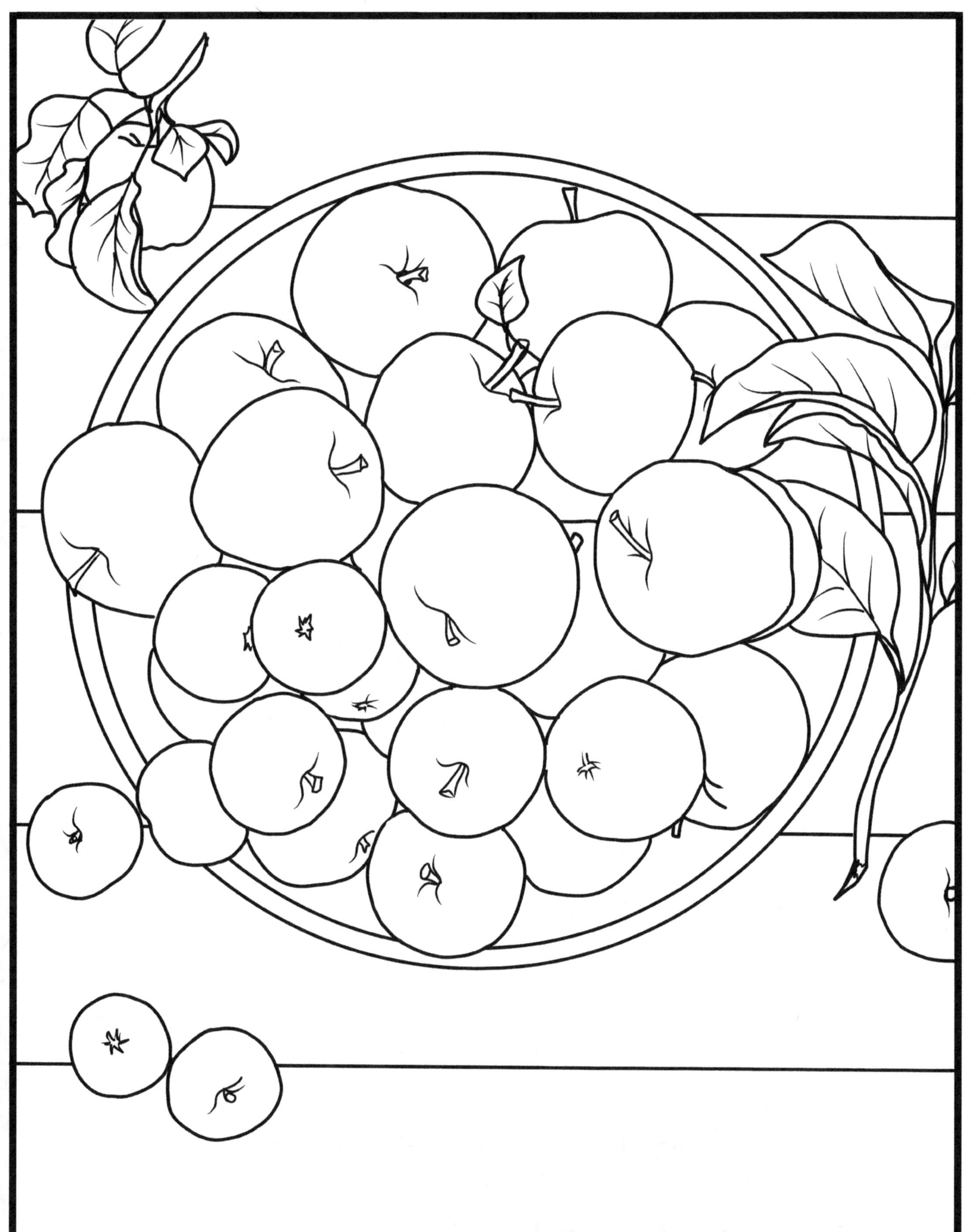

Fresh Apple Harvest

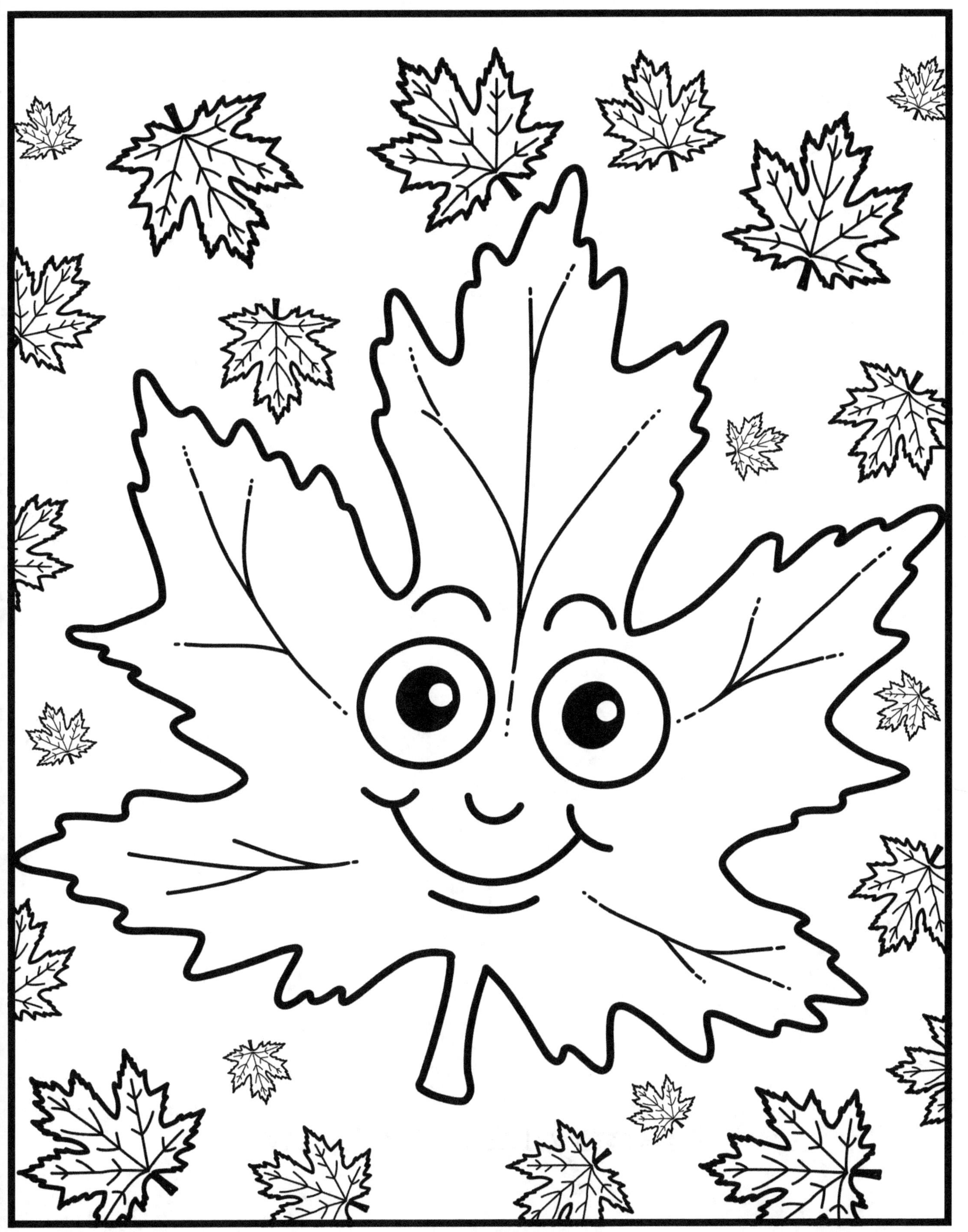

Happy Maple Leaf

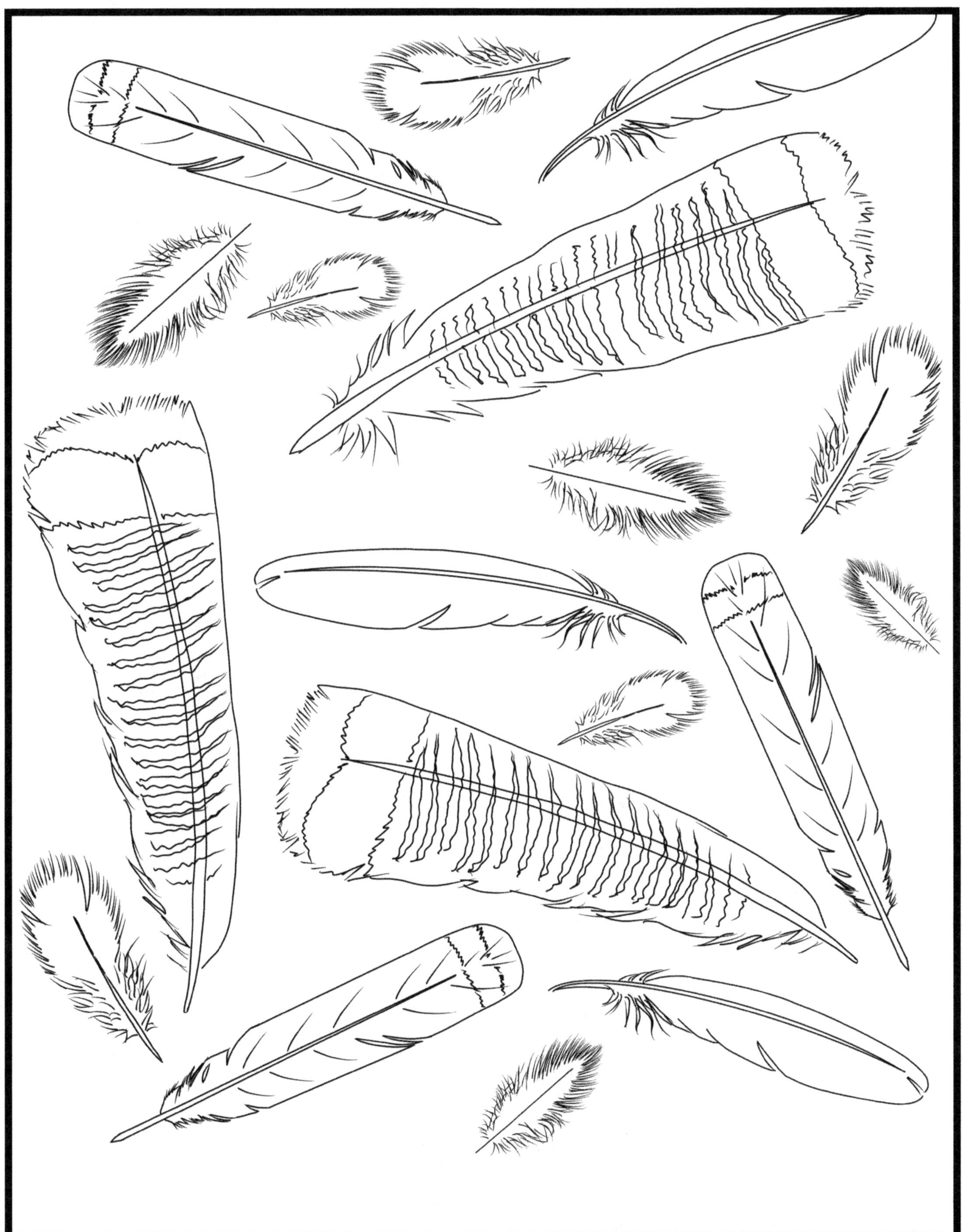

Feathers

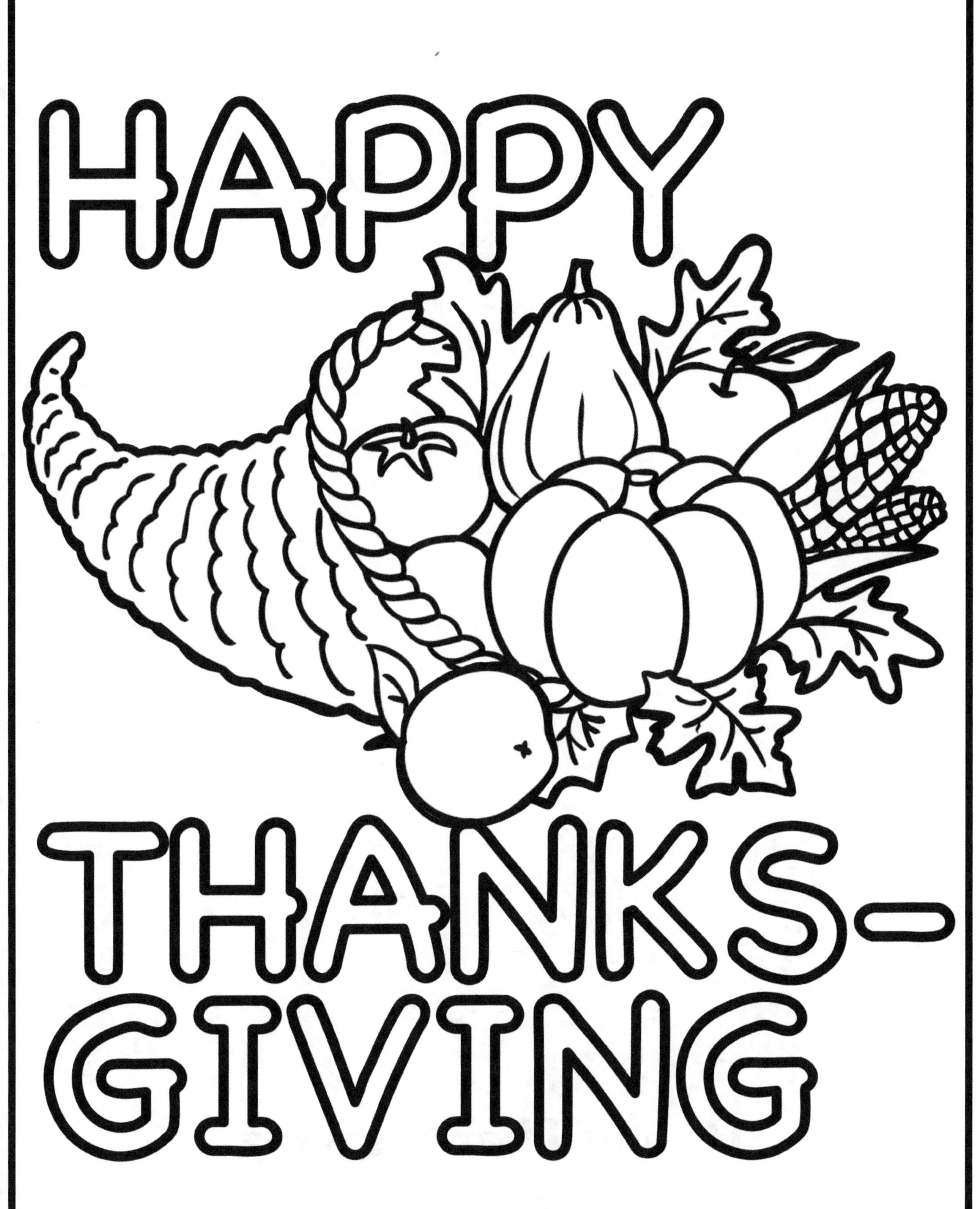
HAPPY
THANKS-
GIVING

Happy Thanksgiving

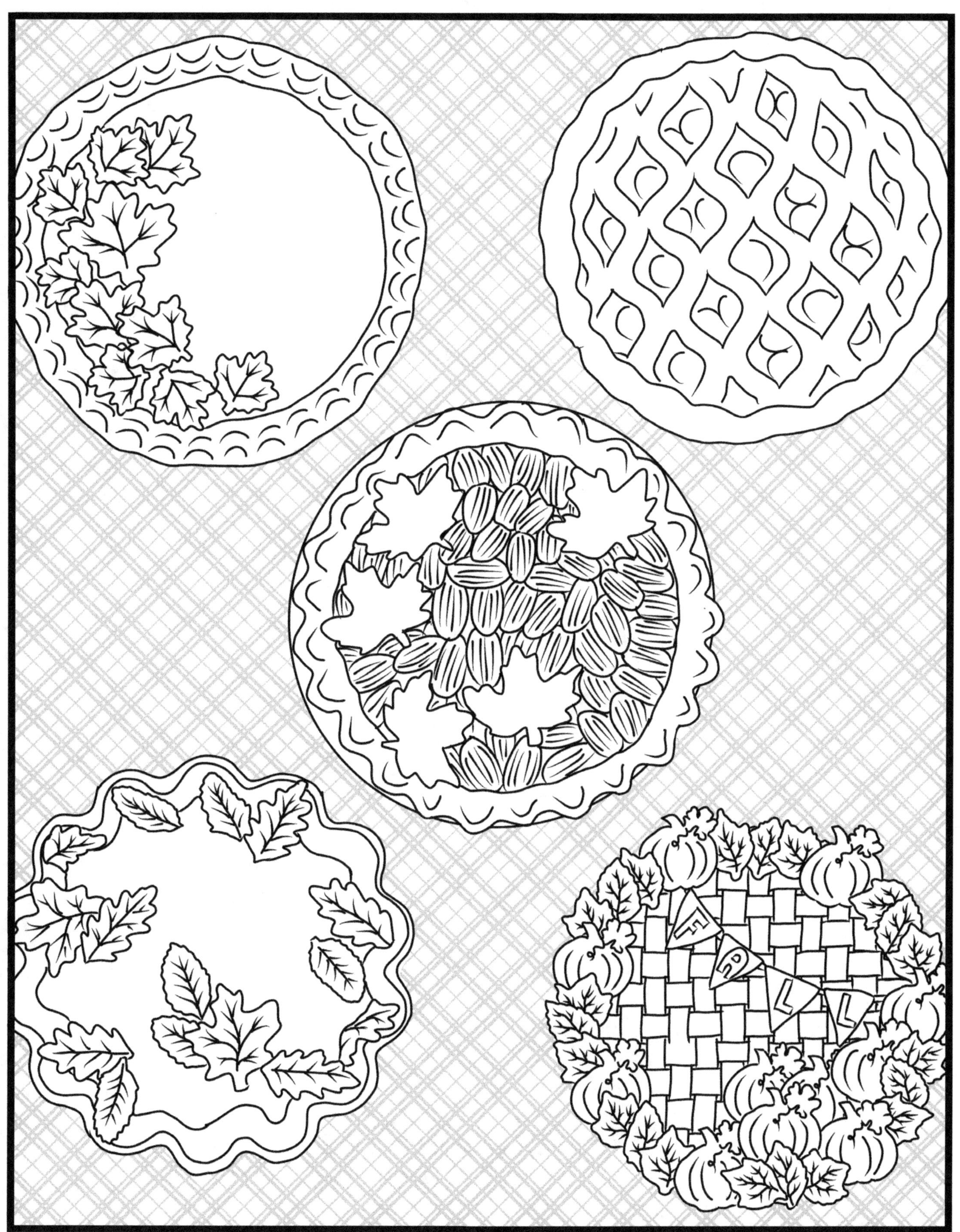
FALL

Delicious Pies

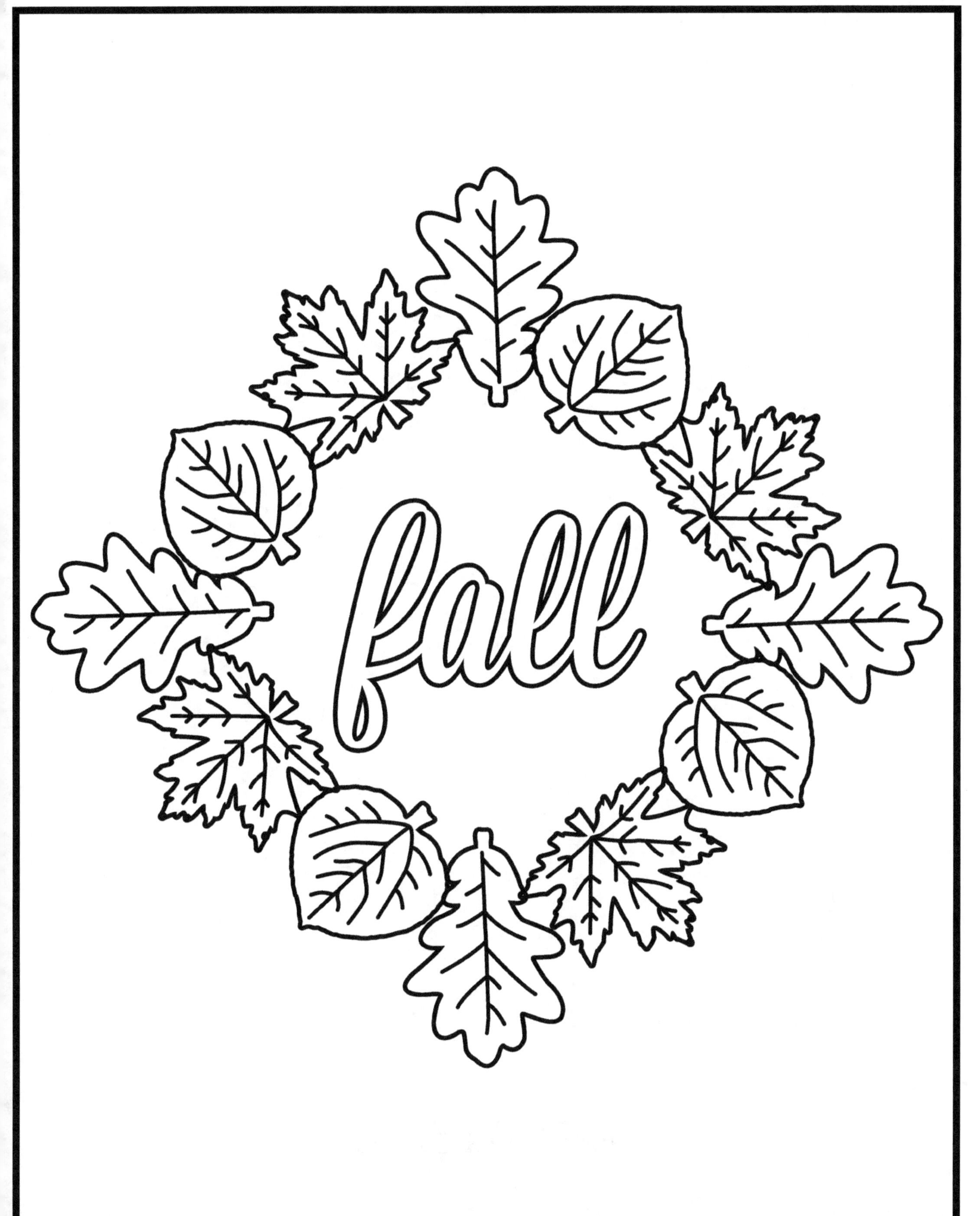
fall

Fall Wreath

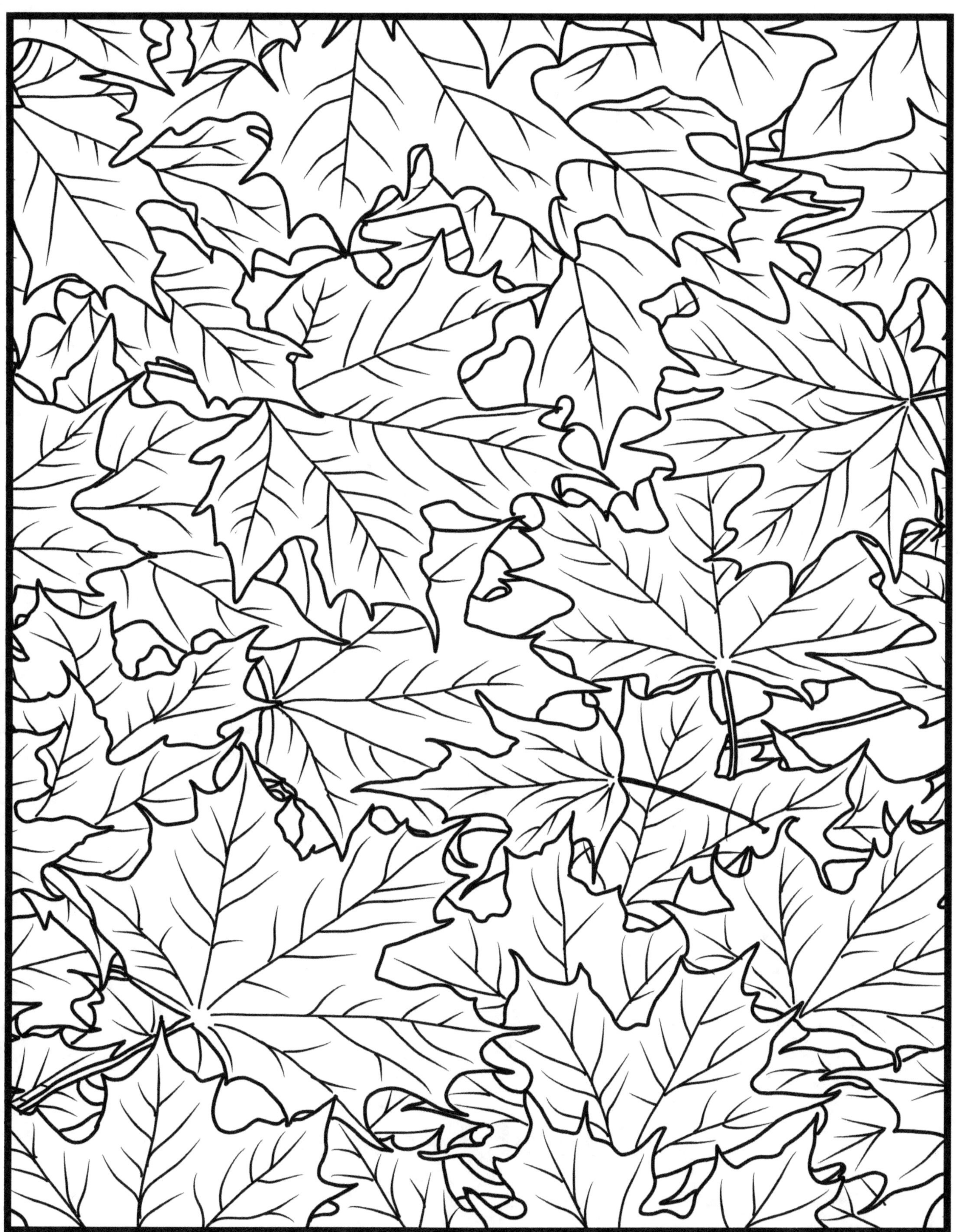

Pile of Leaves

This is Fall

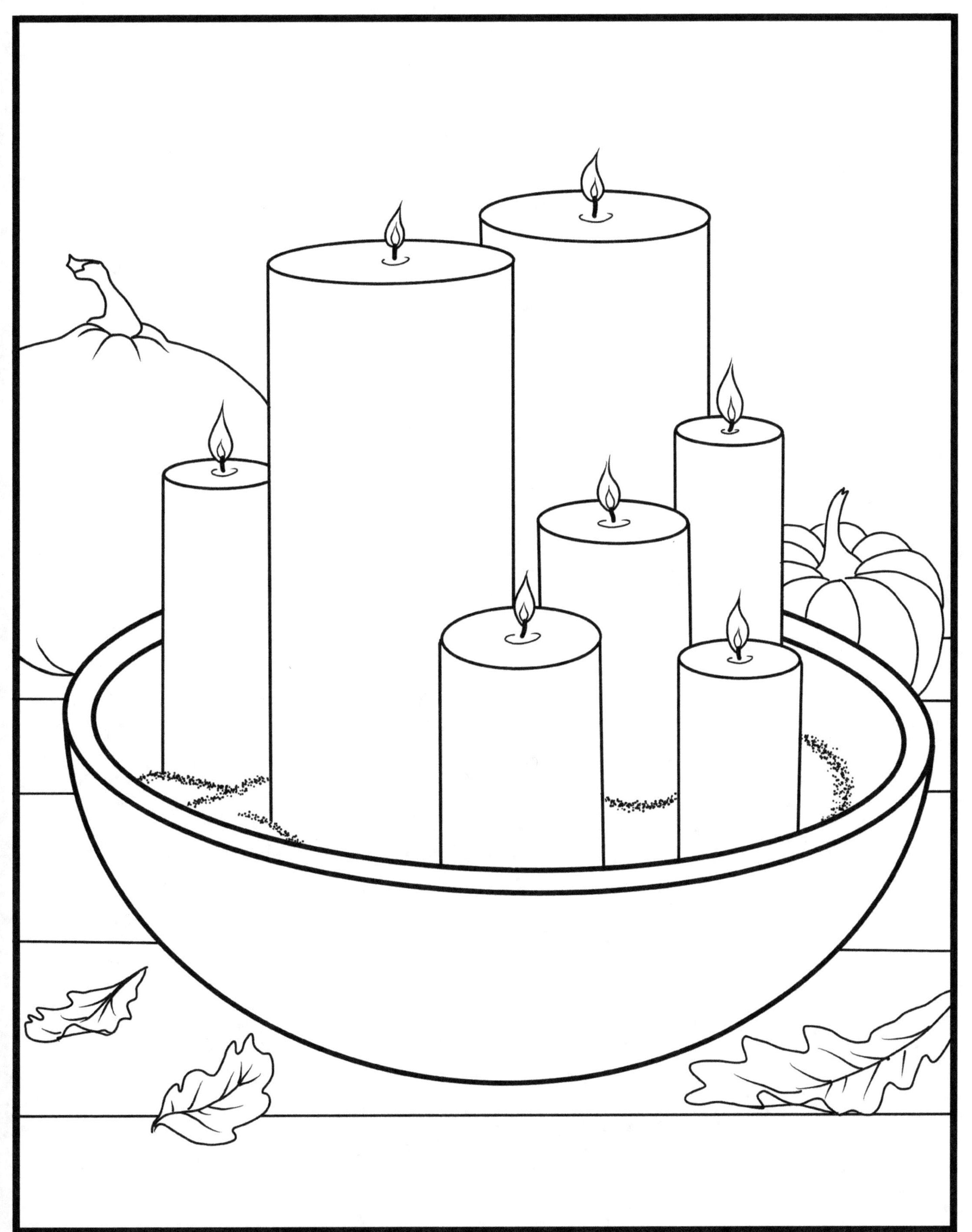

Pillar Candles

Thankful

Grateful

Peaceful

Very Full

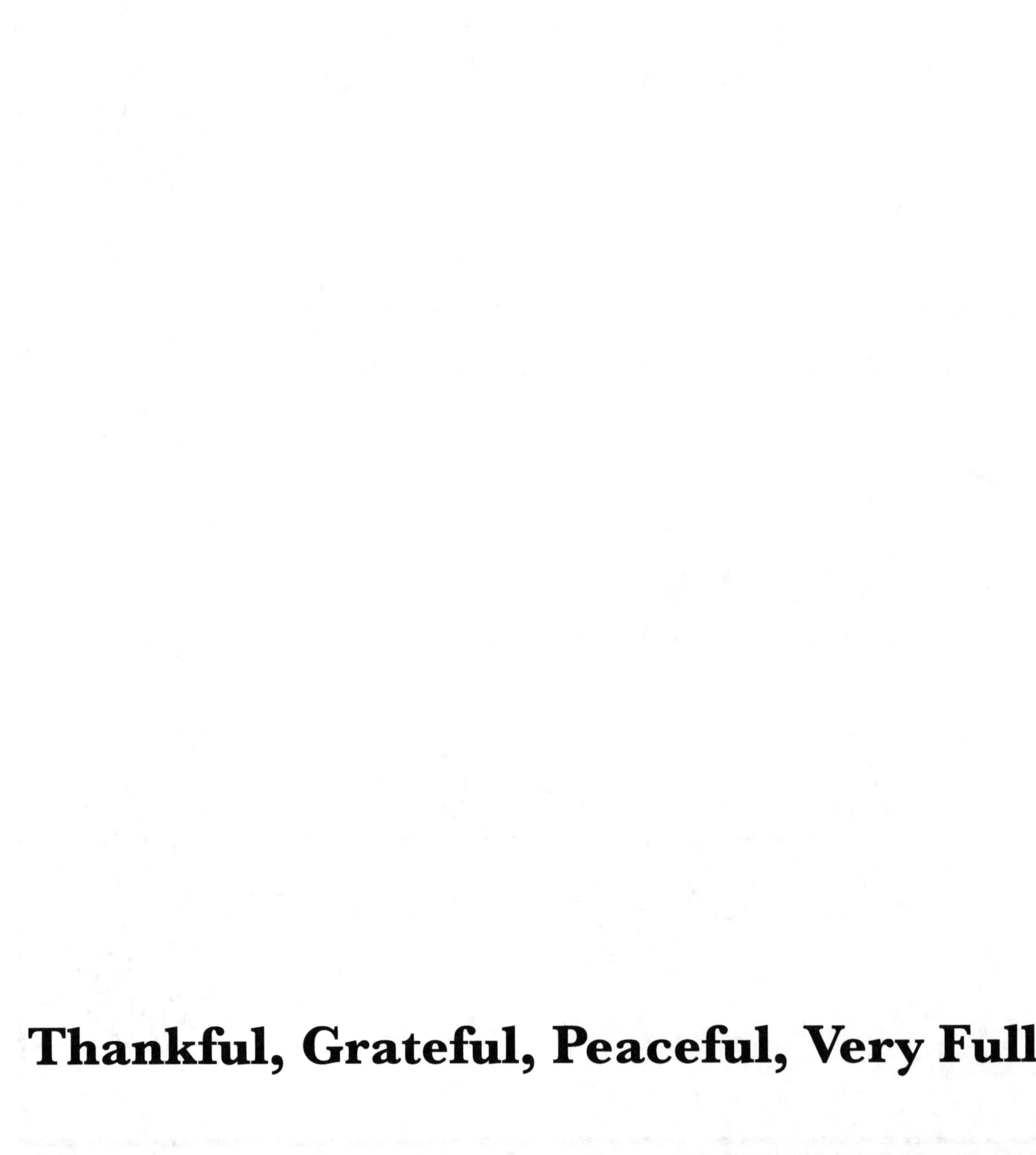

Thankful, Grateful, Peaceful, Very Full

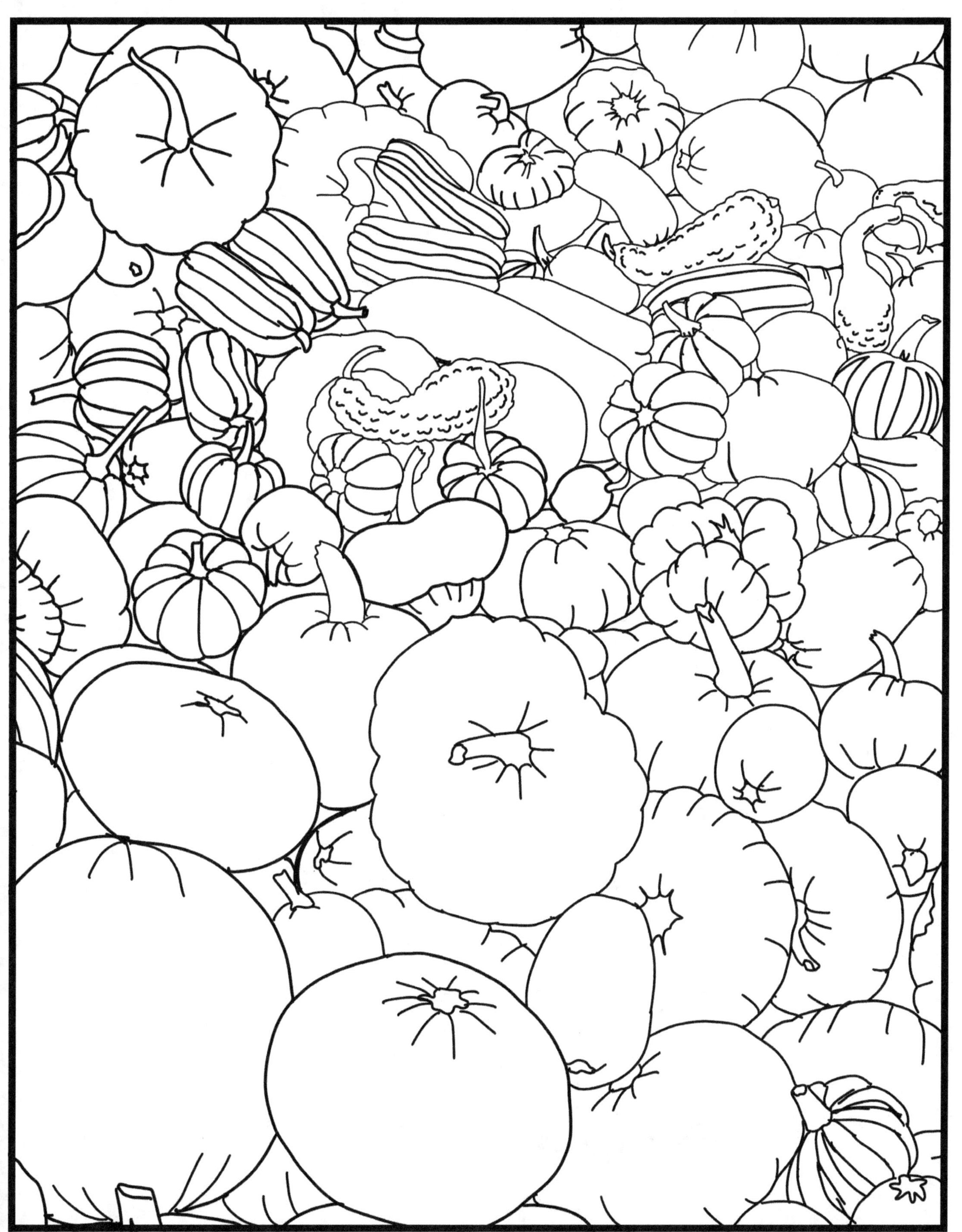

Pumpkins & Gourds

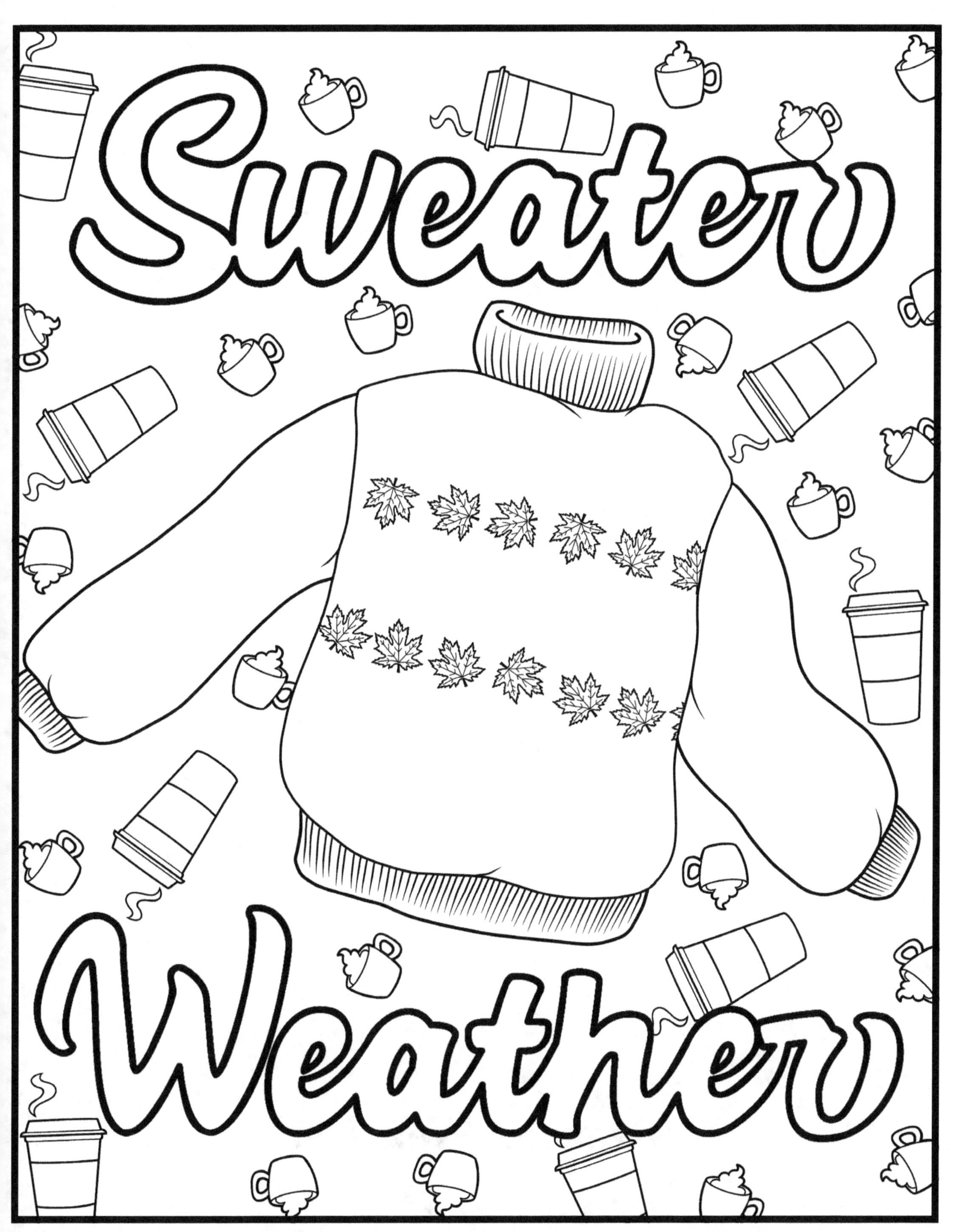
Sweater
Weather

Sweater Weather

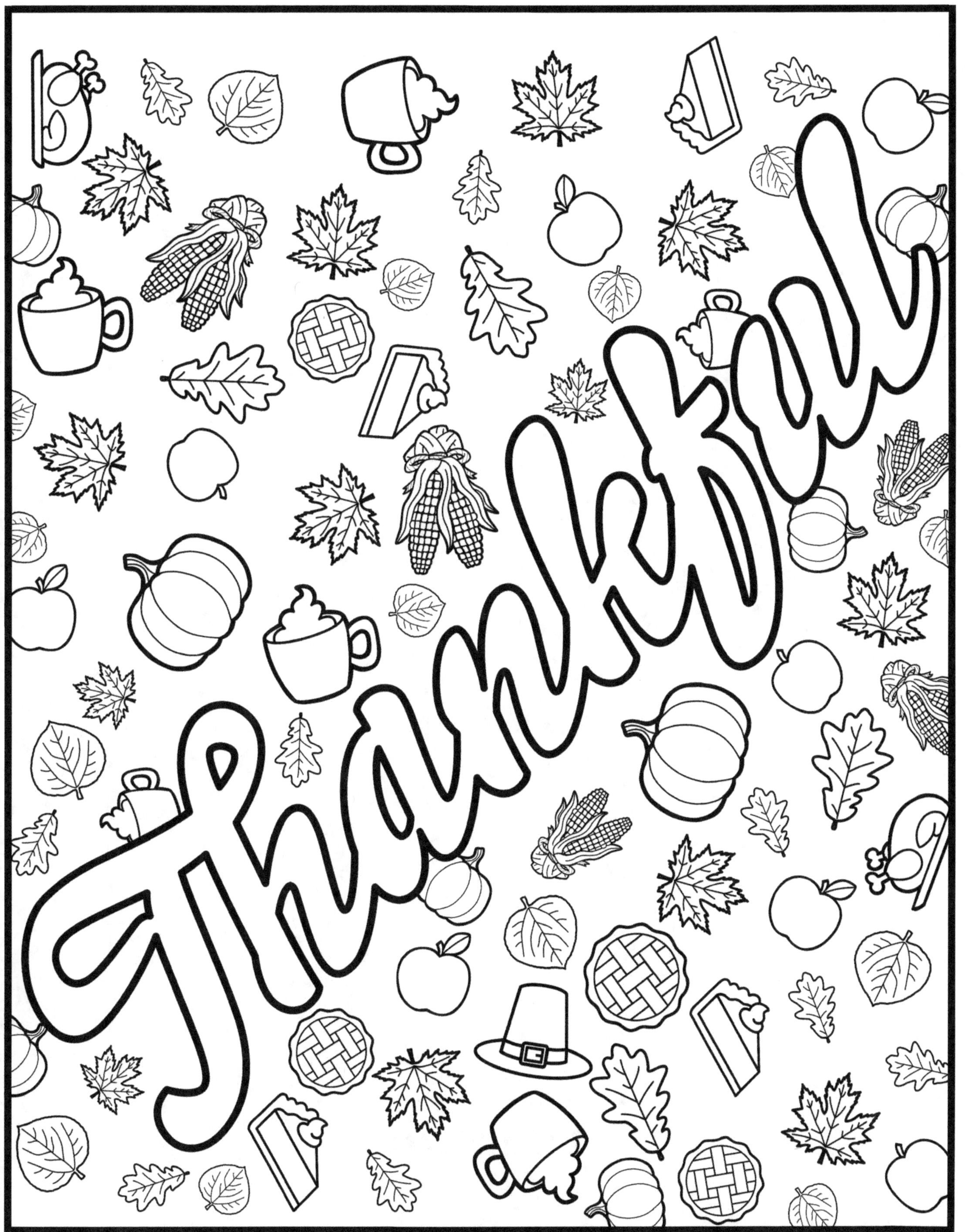
Thankful

Thankful

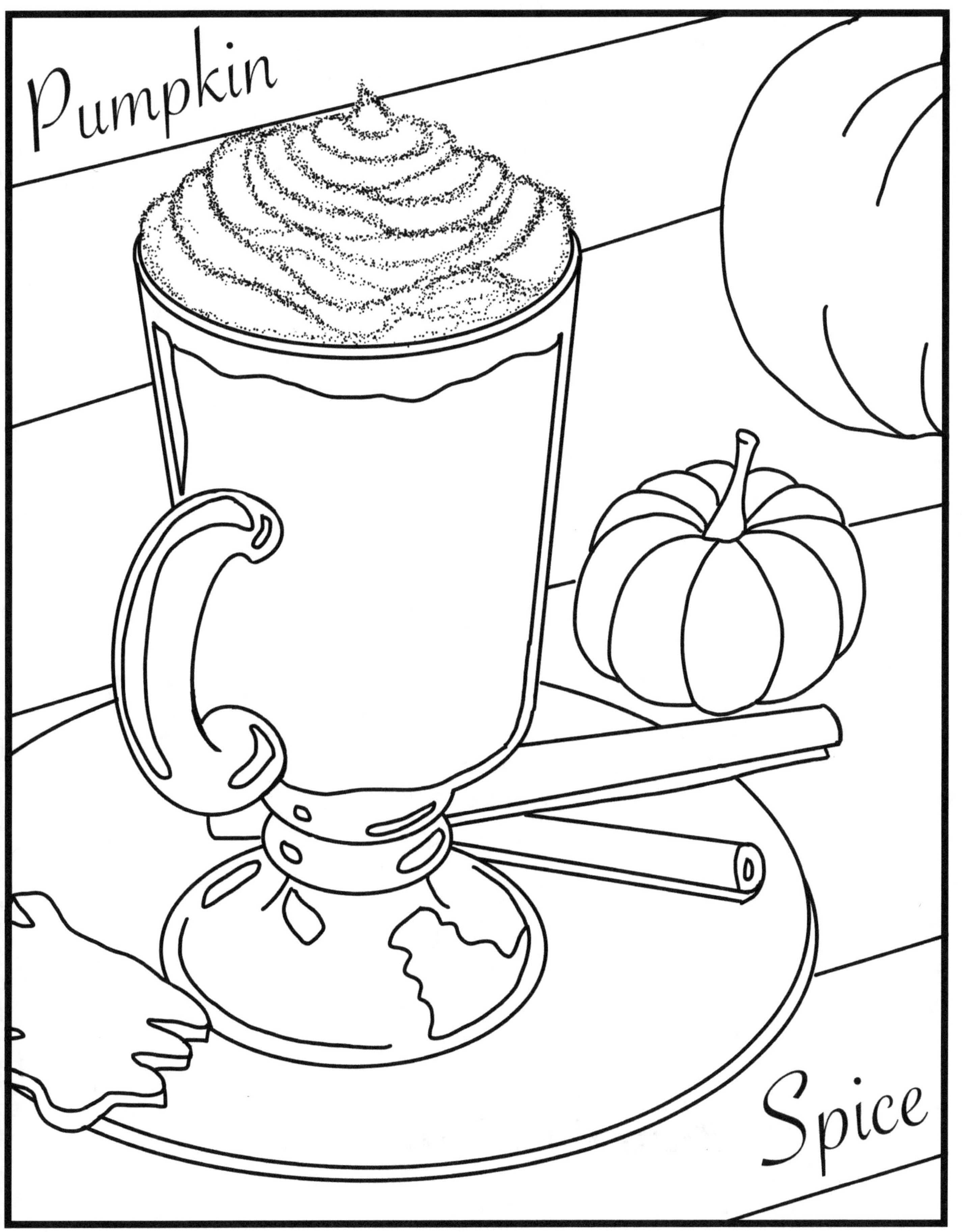
Pumpkin
Spice

Pumpkin Spice Latte

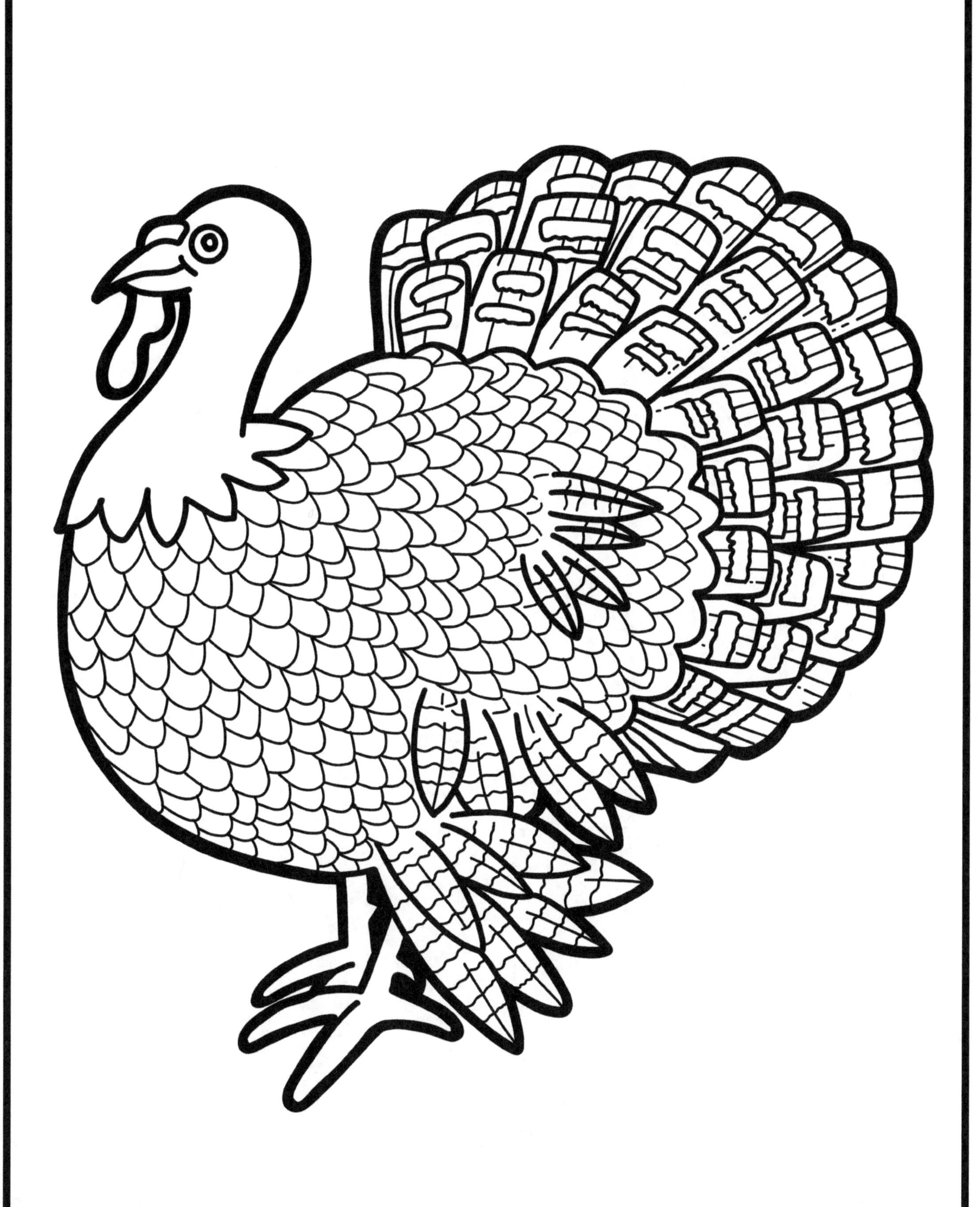

Turkey

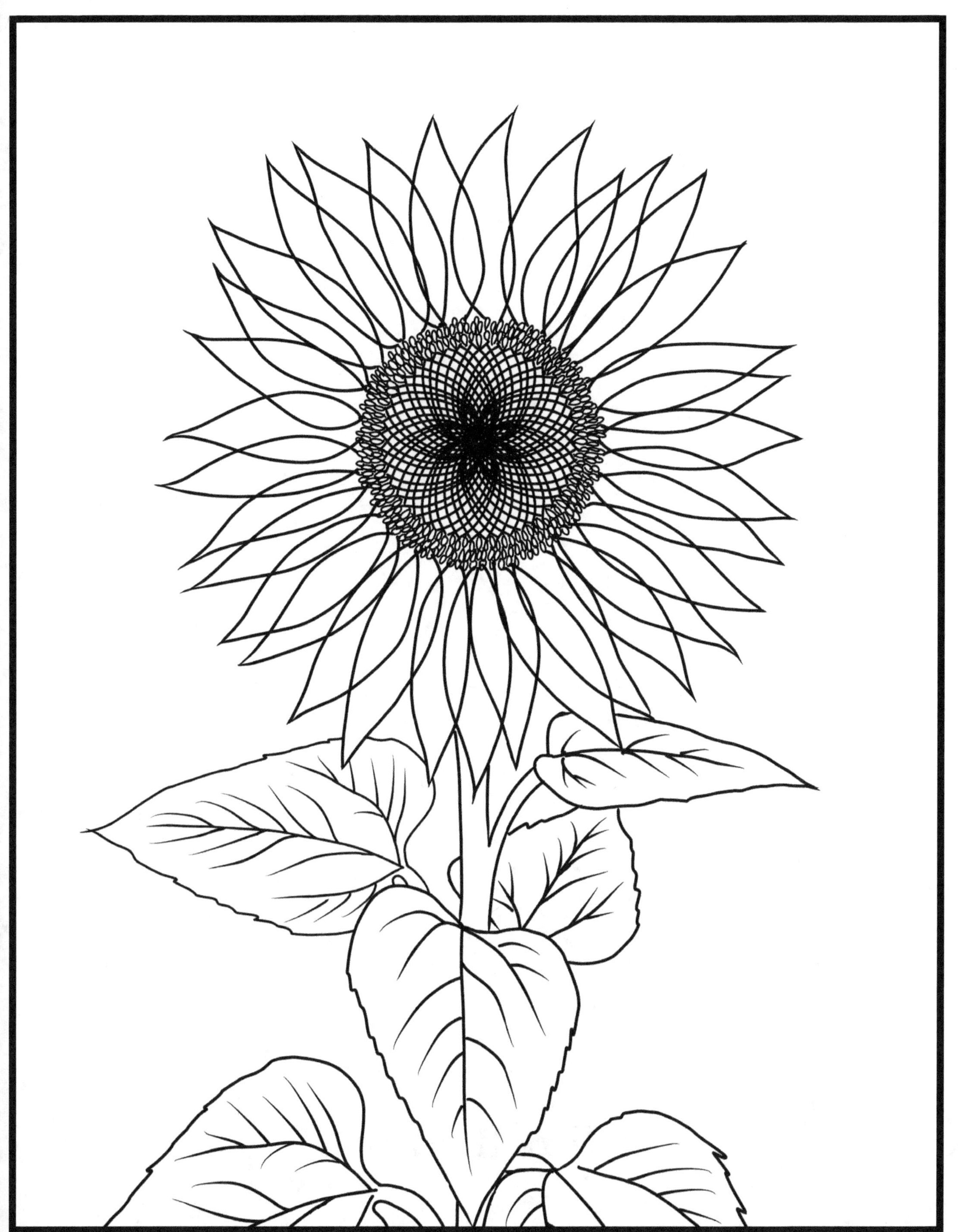

Sunflower

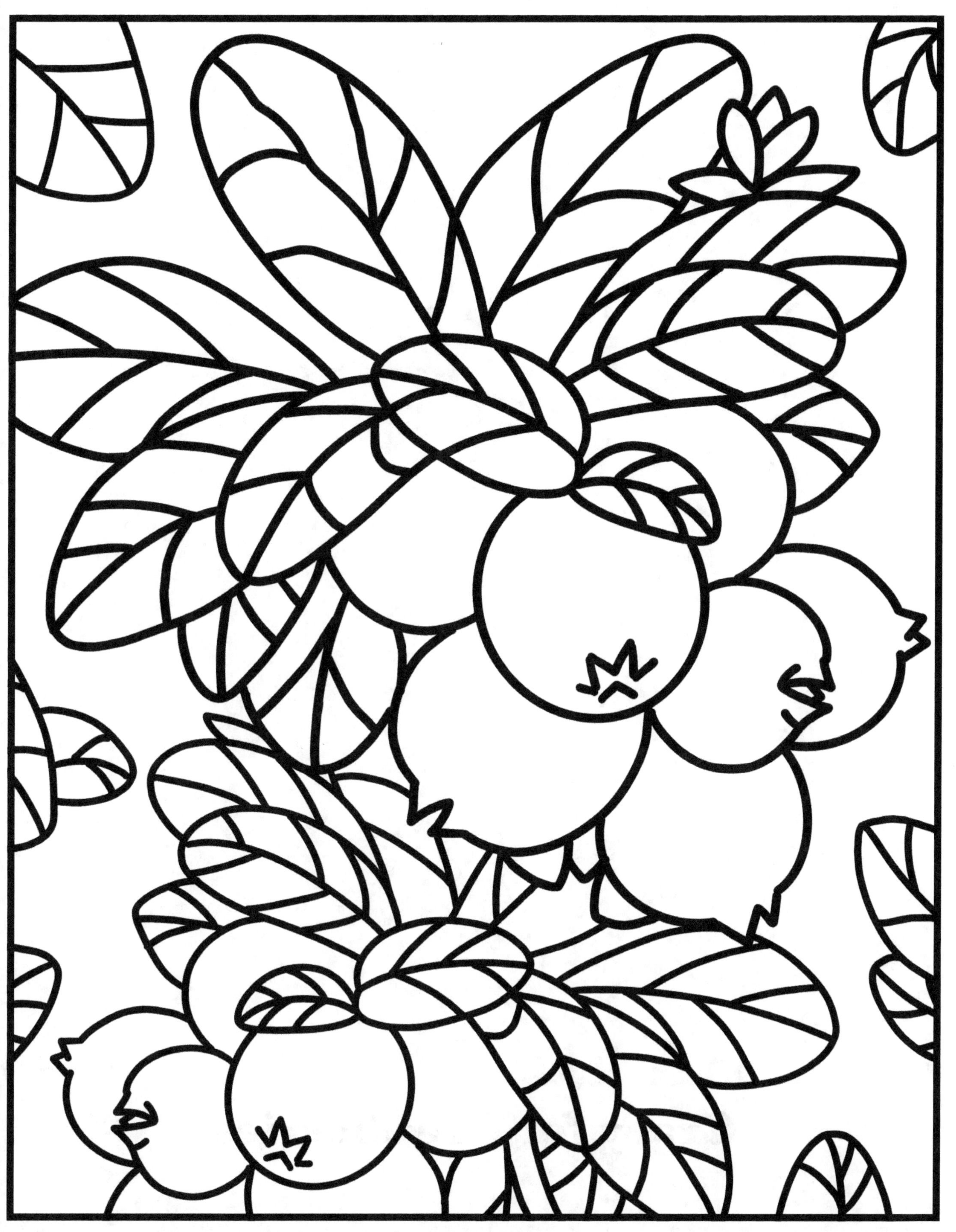

Crazy for Cranberries

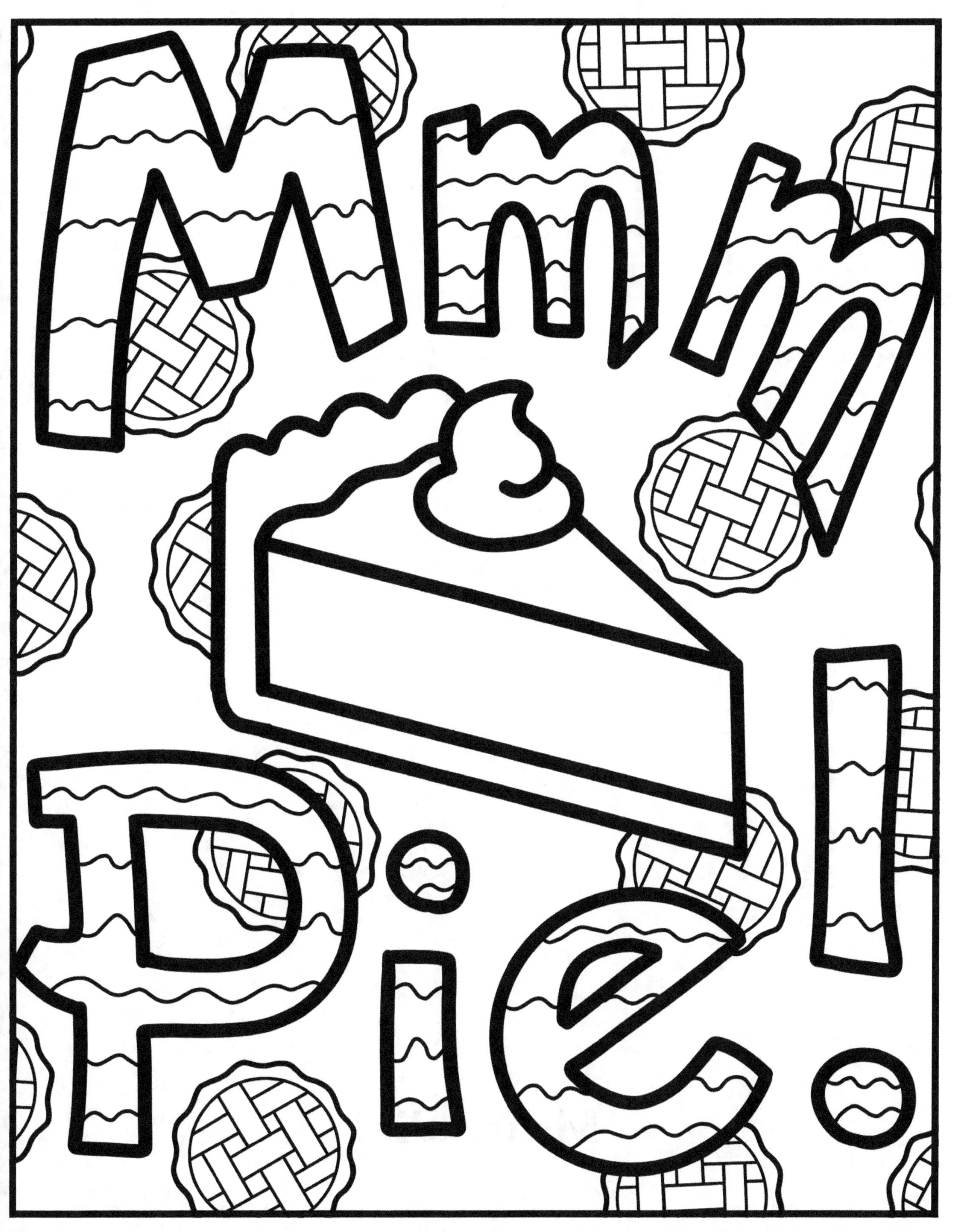
Mmm Pie!

Mmm Pie!

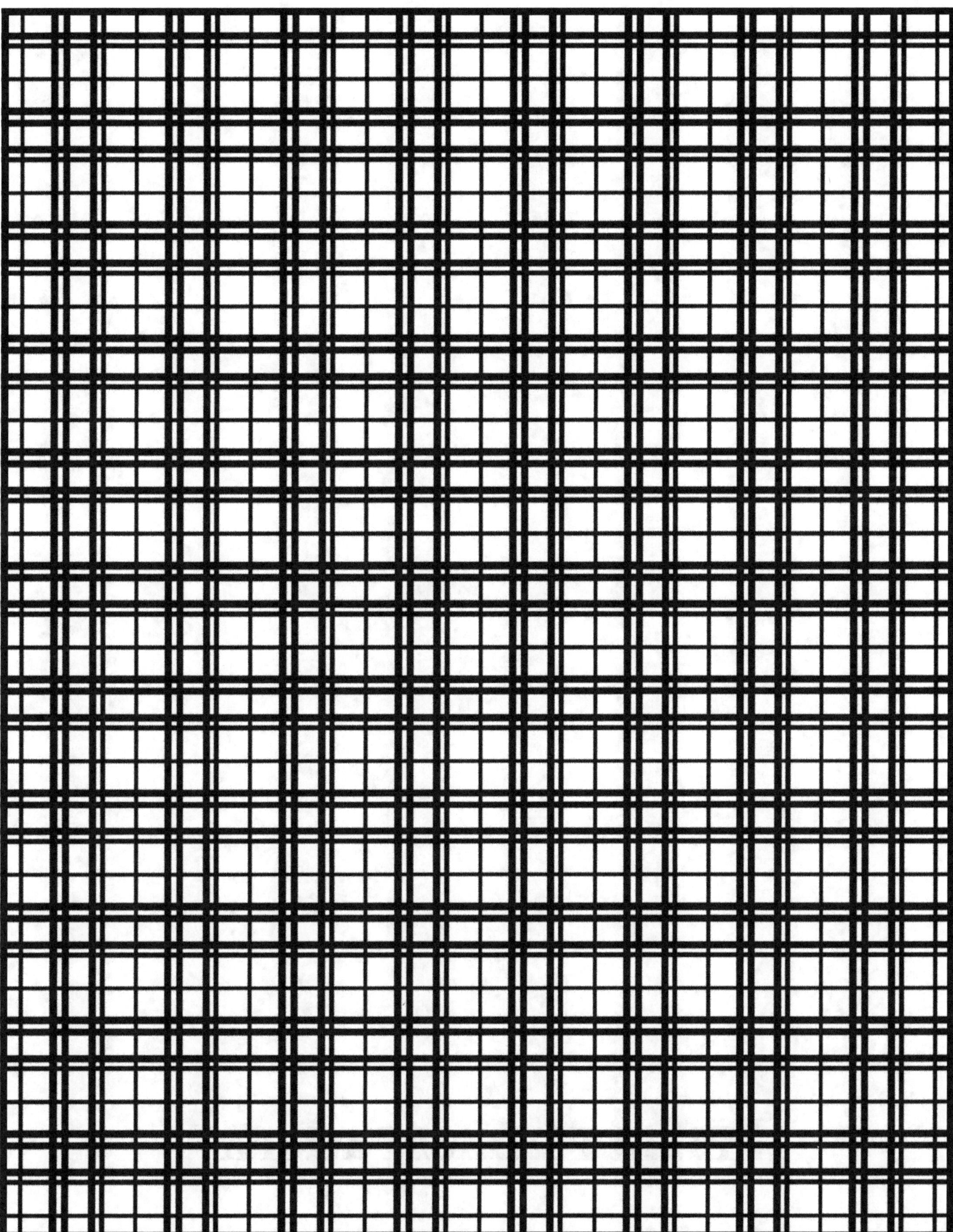

Plaid Flannel Pattern

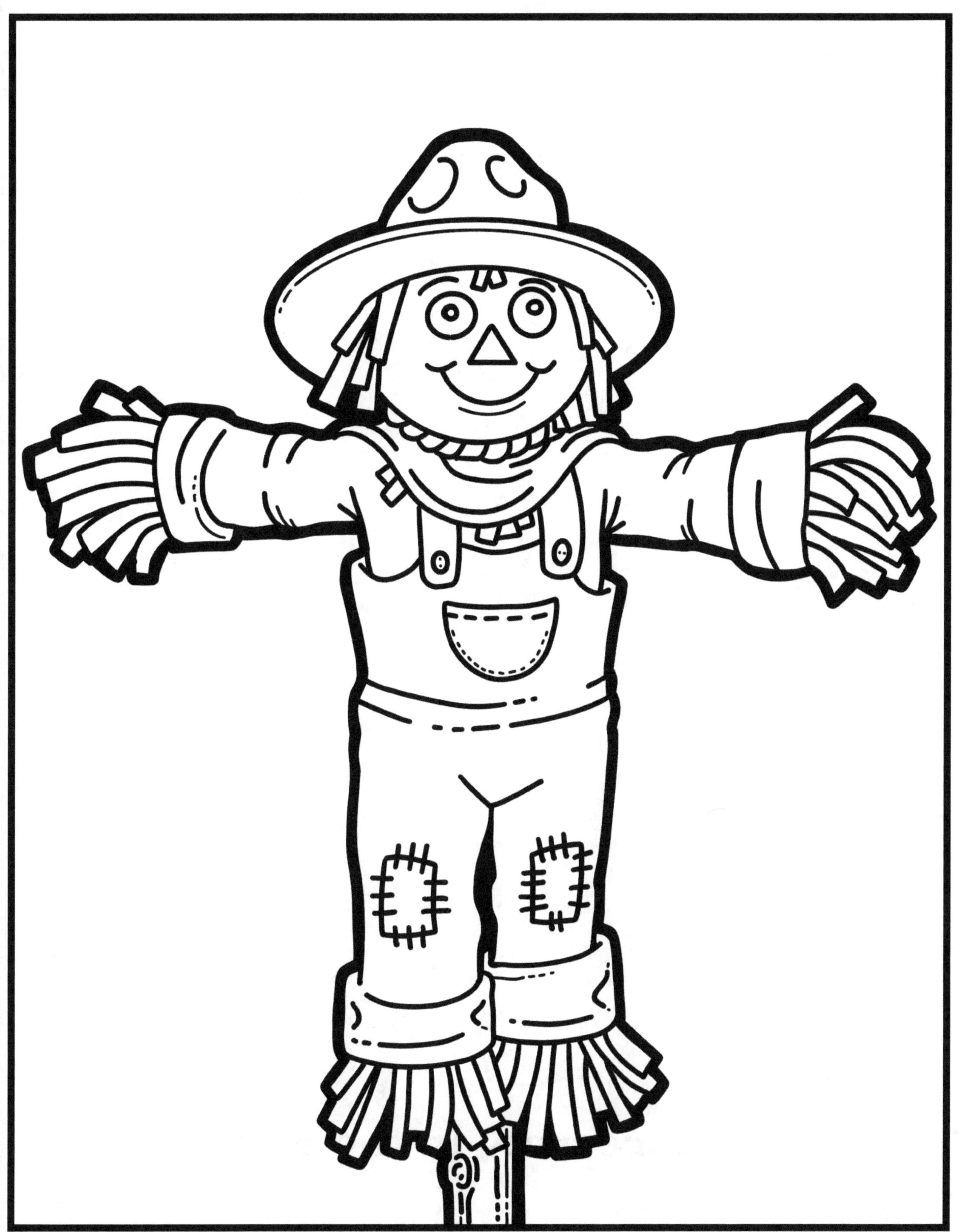

Scarecrow in the Fall

www.ingramcontent.com/pod-product-compliance
Lightning Source LLC
LaVergne TN
LVHW080206180826
845678LV00023BA/1757

9798560780241